It's Easy To Play Ballet Music.

Wise Publications
London/New York/Sydney

Exclusive Distributors:
Music Sales Limited
8/9 Frith Street, London W1V 5TZ, England
Music Sales Pty. Limited
120 Rothschild Avenue, Rosebery, NSW 2018 Australia

This book © Copyright 1983 by
Wise Publications
ISBN 0.7119.0287.9
Order No. AM 32939

Art direction by Mike Bell
Cover illustration by Brian Grimwood
Arranged by Frank Booth

Music Sales complete catalogue lists thousands
of titles and is free from your local music
book shop, or direct from Music Sales Limited.
Please send a cheque or postal order for £1·50 for postage to
Music Sales Limited, 8/9 Frith Street, London W1V 5TZ.

Printed in England by
Eyre & Spottiswoode Limited, Margate, Kent

March

from Casse Noisette

Tchaikovsky

Swan Lake Waltz

from Swan Lake

Tchaikovsky

Pizzicati

from Sylvia

Delibes

Barcarolle Waltz

from Tales Of Hoffman

Offenbach

13

14

Coppélia Waltz

from Coppélia

Delibes

A7

G

Gdim

D7 tacet _ * G

cresc.

f

cresc.

Cm6

G

Cm6

f p

G tacet _ _ _ _ _ _ _ _ _ _ _ _ _ _ _ _

rall e dim.

p a tempo

_ *

Valse Des Fleurs

from Casse Noisette

Tchaikovsky

Russian Dance

from Casse Noisette

Tchaikovsky

Sleeping Beauty Waltz

from Sleeping Beauty

Tchaikovsky

Moderately with expression

35

You And You

from Die Fledermaus

Johann Strauss Jr.

Dance Of The Sugar Plum Fairy

from Casse Noisette

Tchaikovsky

Dance Of The Hours

from La Gioconda

Ponchielli

ENTRANCE OF THE HOURS OF DAY

Andante

DANCE OF THE HOURS OF DAY

Moderato

ENTRANCE OF THE
HOURS OF TWILIGHT

46